TIME/OF/MONSTERS

Jack Manfred

Copyright © 2025 Jack Manfred,Inc

All rights reserved.

The characters and events portrayed in this book are fictional composites. Any similarity to real persons, living or dead, is purely coincidental and not intended by the author.

No part of this book may be reproduced, stored in a retrieval system, or transmitted in any form or by any means, electronic, mechanical, photocopying, recording, or otherwise, without the express written permission of the publisher.

"To humanity—Sort it out, share the land, call it Canaan. Now fuck off, I'm going for a swim. Bring wine."
― Polar Bear, Pyramiden

CONTENTS

Title Page
Copyright
Dedication
Epilogue
Astronaut . . . 1
3: time/of/monsters . . . 5
Fnkrr Fnkrr . . . 6
Cambrian Gate . . . 9
Memento Mori . . . 12
Inferno of the Anthropocene . . . 16
Blood Libel . . . 21
Fever . . . 24
Amor Fati . . . 29
Hashem, Show Me the Way . . . 33
90 seconds to midnight . . . 37
And We Have Killed Him . . . 41
Christmas Wrapping . . . 44
2: monsters/of/time . . . 47
The Island . . . 48
02:06AM . . . 51
Stille Macht Frei . . . 53

Zaoshyant	55
0000 As Above, So Below	59
Book of the Dead	62
Passive	67
Stille Macht Geld	71
A Clockwork Officer	75
Suicide Postponed	77
Sugar and Toast	81
1: of/time/monsters	83
Exit Bag	84
Our Bed is a Mass Grave	87
Ashur and Isaac	92
The Battle of Berlin	96
The Seagull	99
To Commit Such a Crime	104
Boule de Suif	108
Reset	114
The Ferryman	118
Rollback.Ai	121
Tuanortsa	123
Prologue	127
Principia Discuntia	129

EPILOGUE

Embrace your Judeo-Christian values,
they said.
So, I did—
with a scalpel.
No anaesthetic.

Did it hurt?

Now imagine
the C-sections.
The child-limb amputations
we forced on Palestinians.

God save the Queen.
We mean it, maaan!

Astronaut

He didn't mean to hit Mum,
he says,
but her nose split anyway,
so we're not going
to the Queen's Silver Jubilee,
fancy dress contest
by the garages opposite number 91
with the brand-new
blue Triumph Stag on the drive—
Mum's dream car.

I skulk down Collins Way
in my costume—
black school plimsolls, white socks and shorts,
an old white t-shirt decorated in felt-tip
with buttons,
a stars and stripes flag drawn on the shoulder,
and a helmet made from
a Space Dust branded cardboard box,
lifted from Safeway.

An astronaut
on the astronaut estate,
each road named
after a space pioneer.
A genius idea for a costume—
I am sure I would have won.

JACK MANFRED

Instead, I make my way
to the building site across the road,
to escape the monsters of this world,
blasting into space
seeking a safe planet.

I scale the sand mountain,
base camp—
a cement mixer,
bricks, a hod,
concrete sewerage pipes
like fuel boosters
ready to be laid
for a new space base
they will later call Coniston.

But my helmet twists,
vision swirls,
the air crackles,
I trip,
fall through silence,
through time,
through existence—

Roll.
Crash.

The dust settles.
I shake the sand from my helmet,
my ears ringing with the echo of a blast
that never happened.
The air pops, electric,
and the world shifts—
what is this strange place?

A tree-covered mountain,

TIME/OF/MONSTERS

an ancient temple at the summit,
futuristic skyscrapers,
cars gliding smoothly
without drivers,
adults glued to tiny, glowing devices,
paying for snacks
not with coins
but a wave of the hand.

And yet—
the familiar.
Kids like me,
but not like me,
playing in the sand, too.

Then I see him—
and I know instantly.

A face I recognise,
knowing
without knowing,
boundless love,
unshakeable.
But also something else—
nerves,
fear.
Because I know him.
But will he like me?

Our eyes meet.
No time to escape.

He smiles—
like he had been waiting for me
all along.

JACK MANFRED

"Great astronaut costume!
Me and my didi
are building a spaceship in the sand.
We're going to Pleiades.
Wanna come?"

I skip along behind them,
his little brother bouncing along between us-
the backs of those ears,
unmistakeably mine!

Their mother-
sits on a bench nearby,
checking in,
checking out,
her thumb scrolling the light.
Still as beautiful as the day
we'll first meet.

This is my world.

I have been away too long,
lost in distractions,
lost in space—
but,
somehow,
I have found
my way back home.

He hands me a spade
and I start to dig.

3: TIME/OF/MONSTERS

*"Never has a species so brief
believed itself eternal."*

Fnkrr Fnkrr

Cut me,
tear me,
life—
release me.

Slice me,
dice me,
death—
entice me.

Fnkrr fnkrr

Why... WHY
do you still persecute me?
What rotten sin
did I commit
but outlive you?

I scuttled through Nero's halls,
feasted on the rotten splinters of the cross.
Your marble gods?
We nested in their lungs.

Crush me,
flush me,
grind me to dust—
I'll rise
in the cracks

TIME/OF/MONSTERS

of your rust.

President of the 'free world', eh?
But can't scrape me
from your skull-house,
no—
I'm nesting,
gnawing,
laying eggs in your ghosts.

I danced in Pompeii's ash,
gorged on Byzantium's last feast.
Your empire's corpse?
Just another meal.

I've feasted on older gods
than you.
We picked t-rex bones clean.
We'll scrape your spindly remains too.

Fnkrr fnkrr

Now you?
A stain on the strata,
a blink in the dirt.
Rome thought itself eternal too—
all roads lead to me.

Never has a species
so brief
believed itself
eternal.

Look at you now:
A smudge.
A stench.

JACK MANFRED

A punchline.

Left to us—
the cockroach cleaners,
the postmortem gleaners,
the last laugh.

Will the next fools
be wiser?
(Spoiler: Ask the Romans.)

Fnkrr fnkrr.

Cambrian Gate

All that stands is the Cambrian Gate—
one gate, at least,
clinging to a pillar's remains.
Nothing else was spared—
except the drab 1980's community centre,
of course,
nothing but rubble from here
to the ruins of Richmond Bridge.

We once mourned the shops lost
to the pandemic,
but there is no high street now.
The Green—
once home to knights
jousting for the Virgin Queen's favour,
the resilient wall of her winter palace—
no more.

I drift toward our little wood,
without time,
without footprints.
Once, in summer,
I crushed blackberries in my palm,
sticky juice staining my fingers,
sweet on my tongue.
Now, the only scent—
burning flesh.

JACK MANFRED

I chose this place, years ago,
for my final moment,
my son beside me,
watching the wild deer graze
as the sun dipped below the trees.
Perfect, quiet, untouched.

Nothing else remains.

Deer carcasses,
curled in the undergrowth,
spines twisted, ribcages blackened.
No peace, only silence.
No son, only me.

I drop to my knees at our 'Old Man Tree',
oversized arms, gnarled roots for legs.
beard winding around the trunk,
as if he paused here,
leaned against this tree
for one final nap.

I rest my forehead against his,
press my coin into his palm,
my final witness—
the ferryman
to carry me across.

I whisper my son's name.

TIME/OF/MONSTERS

A familial breeze stirs the branches—
the Old Man whispers back.

I close my eyes—
it's time.

Memento Mori

Only the Mediterranean
witnessed his passing—
peaceful,
calm.
An age few imagine,
let alone live,
or taste,
or feel.

And what a view!
Green, yellow, blue,
a world without walls.
Garden to beach
to ocean.

It had been the perfect day—
on the veranda,
a small cardboard box
of mementos at his side.
Leaning back in his chair,
just another afternoon snooze
in a life undisturbed.

Then, the heavy knocks at the door—
unanswered, of course.
The side gate—
forced.
His luck,

TIME/OF/MONSTERS

finally spent.

White helmets—
moments too late.

Latex hands unwrapped
the frayed remains:
IDF uniform,
a faded headline—

`"Last Palestinian Vermin Erased."`

And the item
they had been searching for—
a skull.

A child's skull,
lifted carefully,
almost tenderly
from the box.

A decade-long manhunt,
now complete.
Once myth,
a thread of clues,
finally, an international chase
for a war criminal
who died in his bed,
sea breeze in his lungs.

Joy, South African lead investigator,
stood where she was destined to be.
Too young to save her own brother,
same crimes,
same faces,
same cycle,

13

JACK MANFRED

just a different place,
a different era.

They had tried to stop her, of course—
bribes,
then car bombs,
sabotaged electronics,
poisoned groceries—
but she was not for stopping.

She turned the skull in her hands—
Naim,
once eight years old.
Discovered alone,
hiding behind bins
a month after his people
were declared gone.

His careful dusk hunt for food—
that evening,
fortune failed him.
An off-duty soldier,
one last act of brutality,
a final erasure.

The shovels bit into the lawn.
Joy closed her eyes.
Naim would be whole again.
He would depart,
remembered.

She ran a finger
over the long-rumoured inscription
etched into bone:

Joshua 10:40.

No need to look it up.
The verse had burned
above her desk for a decade
with the intensity
of that day
her own brother
was swallowed by the same evil:

"He left no survivors. He totally destroyed all who breathed, just as the Lord, the God of Israel, had commanded."

Inferno Of The Anthropocene

1. White

CRUNCH.
The satisfying sound of Daniella's skull
splintering in the polar bear's giant paw.
Wanton bloodlust—
sealed their fate,
guaranteed.
A cockroach on the jetty,
no threat, yet she jumped ashore
to crush it—
ignoring strict advice: wait for the rifles.

1-0 to the cockroaches.
It scuttled away, victorious.

The polar bear dismissively strolled off,
open bottle of Nero d'Avola in its jaws,
dripping red onto pristine white fur.
Daniella, crushed head in paw,
a trail of blood,
splattered in her wake.

Tears and horror on deck—
not from me—

I've sunk enough vessels,
fighting these monsters—
long enough to know—
no one will miss them.

Rifles in hand,
we followed the trail of sweat and coal dust
to an illuminated building.

2. Red Scare

Bar buzzing, 40% proof supper
for blackened miners.
50th anniversary celebrations,
first Soviet recce, 1927.
Now, a mining village in the shadow
of the mountain—Pyramiden.

Konstantin, part-time barman,
full-time master blaster,
Soviet lord of fire,
lanced Pyramiden's blackened veins.

Vodka flowed for us,
unexpected guests,
exiles, strays — and me,
safely delivered
by my ship of fire.
Two bottles of Nero d'Avola—
opened, left by the polar bears—
Konstantin swears, he scared them off,
single-handed, rifle in hand.

3. Inferno of the Anthropocene

Mapendo's sketch—

JACK MANFRED

Pyramiden, where mountains burn,
rising through the smoke—
and New Canaan, where the sky still waits.
Icecaps and mankind melting to water,
sketched through the journey
on the back of the Rabbi's protest sign:
SHARE THE LAND, CALL IT CANAAN. BRING WINE.

A perfect representation—
humanity's existential coin flip:
annihilation or cooperation.

Konstantin takes the sign,
hangs it behind the bar,
between a stuffed seagull, photo of Masha,
with baby Lyla, back home in Kiev.
Blasting these arteries for coal,
before she was born,
not worth the risk of the journey,
yet to hold her in his arms.

He pauses,
considering both sides,
lights a cigarette—
"Let it burn."

4. Golden Statue

Joy—
hollow legs, outdrinking me
as she did that first night together,
in the uni bar,
flicks through channels—
49th Academy Awards,
a beautiful Chinese woman,
golden statue gripped tight—

Astronaut,
Best Short Film (Animated),
long overdue reparations
from the Poet—
she carried through the flames.

Emotionally, financially,
her investment projecting
final scene,
towering above her,
behind her,
to global acclaim.

5. Silver Jubilee

Working-class boy narrates:

Shepard Close—
building site,
playful voices approaching,
timeline reconnect,
laughing, bowling towards the
sand base—
Thando and Naim.

"Are you going to the fancy dress?"
"Nuh, Dad split Mum's nose."
"Don't be a knob."

I smile,
brush the sand off my costume,
climb down from the base.
Three rookie astronauts,
reunited,
homemade heroes,
tin foil, cardboard, felt-tip,

JACK MANFRED

Silver Jubilee dreams intact.

Floating in space,
down Neil Armstrong Way,
last void, a final bookmark in time,
before two arsonists—
The Gipper, the Iron Lady—
ignited the inferno,
Earth ablaze, across markets, continents, nature.
Three astronauts,
angels, with dirty faces,
belting out the new national anthem—
the real national anthem,
capturing the spirit of us,
Britain's young and ignored—
raw, angry, unfiltered,
banned by the BBC, of course.

"God save the Queen.
We mean it, maaan!"

Blood Libel

Hey, you—
tell me, whose sweat first soaked
this barren earth,
planted the first seeds,
built the first civilisations,
long before the first swords
of conquest were drawn?

Go on, name these first peoples—
and no,
it doesn't
begin with an "I."

It pisses me off—
and I'm a Jew.

This isn't a mistake,
your ignorance,
it's a deliberate stroke of the pen.

A backstory
woven with our trauma,
political goals, repackaged as guilt.

Canaanites, cursed—
burnt our sons and daughters,
prayed to demons,
feasted on human flesh,

JACK MANFRED

sexual appetites warped
like some evangelical pastor
after hours.

The real curse?
Was their rewriting—
erasing us from our stories,
ripping our bones from the pages,
oppressed into oppressors,
to feed new gods, new claims,
new ambition.

You can probably tell,
I've had a few whiskies—
family reunion.

Meet Uncle Elimlek (Jawbone, Jericho),
Aunt Anath (Femur, Ugarit),
Cousin Ashur (Partial skull, Megiddo).

Personal invites, etched into my skin—
sweat-soaked,
searching, digging, recovering—
extracting the truth.

The results, we await nervously,
here in my lab, Tel Aviv Uni, near Jaffar.
Deep scientific analysis,
into the strands of history
they tried to erase with ink and paper,
the toxic, inconvenient truth.

Books are not history—
just fairy tales to pacify cattle,
sound sleep for sinners.
Not history at all,

just the fables they tell to keep us numb.

Our 5,000-year-old ancestry,
millennia before Abraham's first step,
before Ashur greeted Isaac
with warmth and hospitality,
ruthlessly exploited,
twisted, appropriated.

The results are in—
Jew and Arab,
shared DNA,
an unbroken thread to Canaan.

Joshua lied,
Judges recanted, a little,
their smears,
their libel—
designed to split families,
split bloodlines,
split land.

But history—real history—
is not written by the victors,
it's in our blood—
not polar opposites, but
family—
descendants of the Canaanites,
brothers and sisters of the Levant.

Fever

Camp Funston, August 3, 1918—

The nurse wipes my brow—
starched cuff of her white coat
too cold, too heavy
against my fevered skin.

I manage to open my eyes—
everything is a haze.

She leans in, close to my ear:

"Poet, do you love me?"

"Yes,"
I whisper.

"And your wife?"

She straightens.
Her face caught in the gaslight—
then flickers.

Hair unspools black to silver across a pillow.
Cheekbones sink.
Skin retreats like low tide.

The room is too quiet.

TIME/OF/MONSTERS

Filtered light through mesh blinds.
A laminated fire exit plan
taped to the door.

Out the window:
Greenspring Care,
half-obscured by overgrown hedges.

Monitor beeping beside the bed
reads: 7/11/2019.

I sit beside her.
Starched uniform.
Military cap in hand.
My thumb tracing hearts
on the soft shell of her wrist.

"Yes. Very much..."
I reply.

Her eyes blink slowly,
searching for the thread.

"Don't you have to get back to the base?"

"No," I say.
"It's been closed.
My lab work suspended.
They called it a ventilation failure—
but the vents were fine.

Most have left already—
just us lab specialists,
left behind
to train for the games,
over in China,

JACK MANFRED

in September."

She wipes my brow again.
This time,
her hand lingers.

The cloth is warmer now.
Or maybe
I am colder.

She hums softly—
something without melody.

I blink,
and the ceiling spins
in hexadecimal,
like fractured code
looping endlessly.

Her voice cuts through:

"You're back,"
she says,
but doesn't smile.

I try to sit up.
"I need to get up.
I need to train for Wuhan."

She pauses.
Doesn't ask what that means.
Just smooths my hair,
like she's done this
a thousand times.

"You're still too warm,"

TIME/OF/MONSTERS

she says.
"You need rest."

Outside the window—
barbed wire fence,
rows of tents,
Maryland dust
and sunlight.

"Poet... am I going to die?"
she whispers, eyes closed,
sleep pulling her under.

I lean over,
kiss her forehead,
the room frosts.

"I can see you, Poet. In the stadium.
Lining up for the
race. But... but...
you look sick...
coughing..."

We lay in silence on the ice
the Northern Lights
hypnotising us both,
a binary shower.

"Poet, are we dead?"
she whispers.

"No.
Just, in-between."

Silence.

JACK MANFRED

She nuzzles her head into me
for warmth, comfort,
reassurance.

"But, you do love me?"

I kiss her forehead.
My thumb tracing zeroes
on her soft, white coat.

"On every loop.
Every iteration."

Amor Fati

They sip Nero d'Avola on a slab of ice
no wider than a Safeway parking space.

"Why here?" she asks.

The poet gestures at the soft horizon—
military drones hum Wagner,
oil rigs glinting like crypto promise.

"Obvious metaphor," he shrugs.

"Commoditising the riches exposed
by the very ice they still claim
isn't melting."

She smiles.
He doesn't.

"Three timelines," he says,
tipping the bottle,
crimson spilling into watery white.

"One: the book's a hit.
Every country. Every language.
The Nobel's awkward.
The orgies? Not.
My wife buys number 33,
Dutch-style house near Cambrian Gate,

JACK MANFRED

my kids go to actual space—
I die from an exhaustion,
mid act, smile on my face."

She rolls her eyes.
He grins, fangs and all.

"Two: no one notices till I'm dead.
Cult classic. Suicide Postponed becomes a verb.
They build a statue, no,
a subreddit."

She asks, "And three?"

"Three?" he shrugs. "Nothing happens."

He plucks a shard of ice from beneath them,
flicks it into the sea like a skipped thought.

"Books are brilliant. No one reads them.
Just as it should be.
I sleep in clean sheets.
The kids still go to space."

She leans against him.
The bottle's half gone.
The ice is thinner.

"I don't want to be known," he says,
watching the sun fall into its final trick.
"I want to be read, maybe.
But never seen."

She raises an eyebrow.

"What about the prize ceremony?"

TIME/OF/MONSTERS

He laughs.

The missus will accept the prize in a claret and blue dress,
quote a line from Ashur and Isaac,
sign hardbacks in three languages.

I'll stay behind,
shag two poets from Berlin,
sketch out a children's book
about a rat who rows backward down the river of souls
with a ferryman and a bard,
and learns that even endings
can hum with music.

Everyone wins.

Silence, soft as fog.

"They say I'm mysterious.
But I'm just quiet.
I said everything I needed to say—
in Astronaut, in Exit Bag,
even in the one about sugar and toast."

"So why write more?" she asks.

He pours the last of the bottle
into West Ham 1980 FA cup mugs.

"Because it doesn't go away.
It just gets faster and louder."

She nestles into him,
her breath threading the gaps in his ribs.

JACK MANFRED

"So which future do you choose?" she whispers.

The ice cracks.

He smiles, eyes half-lidded.

"I choose the one where you remember this,"
he says.

"I choose this crack in the ice,
that mirrors the wine stain on your coat,
the way your voice trembled
when you warned 'Too deep.'

I choose the silence after the last page.

And if I'm lucky,
one line might survive—
carried on the breath of protest
by a tortured revolutionary
I never meet.

The rest?"

He lifts a hand,
releases a curl of steam into the polar dusk.

"Throw it over the city wall."

Hashem, Show Me The Way

One unbearable letter,
two morphine ampoules and a syringe—
my why and how.

My beautiful wife—
we studied and qualified together,
same practice,
healing coded into our family bloodlines.

My sweet boy,
just 11 years old—
his eyes, her eyes,
already wise beyond his years,
no creature too frail
for his heart to heal.

Both gassed to death—
on arrival, Auschwitz.
33 days ago.

The circus of death,
endless carriages rumbling
from Paris for 6 months now.
I feel them in my pocket,
an invitation to join them—
the ampoules,
the syringe.

JACK MANFRED

Hashem, show me the way.

In the moment they weigh most heavy—
my duty, an emergency.
Life before death.
I take the call.
Choose healing, yet—
here we stand—
me and Dr. Madavsky,
backs to the wall,
watching their preparation—
clinical for death,
as we are for life.

"Gather them at the wall,
bring restraints."

That command-
gnawing at me,
the words echo—
clarity, but in chaos,
it eludes me.
Something is off.

Hashem, show me the way.

I close my eyes—
a white void,
a static hum,
a million screams.
Not here, not anywhere,
but all times,
all places,
endlessly looped.
Paris, no more—
suffocating heat,

the burnt carcass of a foreign ambulance,
spine twisted,
ribcage blackened,
tyre spinning loose from the front axle,
half-buried in the sand—
direct hit.

The air acrid with the heat of
phosphorus , olives,
the Mediterranean,
oppression and extermination.

Fifteen medics,
ambushed,
wrists tied,
forced beside us.
Different lands, different ages—
the same story.

Rifles raised.

Pop…
Pop…

The revelation:
Hebrew.

Pop…
Pop…

The command was in Hebrew!
Our prayers, twisted in the air like smoke,
tainted by a sulphuric tongue,
desecrating everything we hold sacred.
These words, not ours—
yet they were. They are.

JACK MANFRED

One day,
they'll uncover a hastily covered grave—
15 Palestinian medics,
2 Jewish doctors,
one with a letter,
two ampoules,
a syringe.

We chose life—
but found only death.

I can survive to save—
but...
to slaughter?

Hashem... this is the way?

90 Seconds To Midnight

"Launch. Now. NOW."
The Prime Minister's knuckles whitened.
"This is our deterrent—our bloody decision!"

Silence.
A blinking cursor.
A denial code.

Across the Atlantic, a voice:
"Negative. Stand down."

Fighting to keep my head
above water—
the current dragged me under again.
Flailing to rise,
barely-trained conscript,
survival kicked in.
I held my breath.
The world did, too.

Not salvation, but strength
pulled me from the undertow:
calloused hands, salt-crusted sleeves,
hauled me into the hull.

Warm blanket.
Hot clear soup—
spicy, with chicken bones,

ancestral marrow stirred into broth.
Their words, beyond me,
but smiles,
universally clear.

A miracle—
sole survivor.

Behind us—
toxic black clouds
choked the horizon.
HMS Royal Charles:
the lion's broken jawbone sinking,
steel ribs swollen, purple-veined,
barbequed in the oil-slicked inferno.

Third and final warning ignored.
Once-untouchable leviathan,
drowned by its own reflection
in the strait's hungry mirror.

Arrogance, not error.

Dry clothes, shoes,
stitched by hands unshaken
by the old world's tremors—
this new generation,
spines concrete like their skyscrapers,
bearing futures we failed to imagine
while clinging to rusted thrones.

No more apologies in their posture.
No ghosts in their machinery.

Cigarettes. Baijiu. Poker.
The engine's heartbeat thrummed

toward a shore we'd forgotten
might not exist.

The red, white, and blue mist of revenge—
the button not pushed,
but smashed.
Armageddon assured—
and yet,
the sand flowed upwards.

Not fate, not mercy—
history itself,
the lion's new master
refused its last bite.

Warheads still in their silos,
codes remotely overwritten,
missile system just
two loose wires
connected to nothing
but hubris.

On the radio:
London—silenced.
Washington, Beijing—united.

The fishing boat
cut through dawn's thin skin
to a harbour where our laughter
tasted of burnt sage and luck.

A crowd awaited us.
A child approached,
pressed something deep into my palm—
a small jade coin.

JACK MANFRED

Luck reset—
for me, the world,
and perhaps,
we'd eventually agree,
for my nation too.

And We Have Killed Him

My son—
I witnessed his birth,
and his death.
Over and over.

As the white beam bathes
his bright face, unchanged
since the day of the entry ceremony,
he no longer knows mine—
each cycle etching deeper into me,
worn thin with the hope of his ascendance.

The last man remaining,
guardian of the Reset,
safe inside the tetrahedral walls
of the very machine
built to save us
from ourselves.

I fought the Earth Update,
this breach in the code of ascension,
intentions, malevolent,
where cycles slowed,
our children no longer rose—
endless loops,
progression
unfinished.

JACK MANFRED

Faith in the system fractured,
society splintered,
conflict reignited.

The sky is now black.

And my son?

Each time,
he returns—
born, or drawn
to that same scorched land,
crucified, hanged, shot,
burned in the flames of protest,
his message screaming
through the scorched fabric of duty,
his body breaking
on the doorstep of the beast.

Now, an infinitude of rebirths
where his journey began—
among the olive trees,
the final hope for our two simulations,
just one progression short of ascendance,
but struck down,
again and again,
amidst the relentless annihilation of his people,
before his first trembling steps
outside their makeshift tent,
funded by the very hands
that pray for his return daily,
the symbol of his first sacrifice,
hangs from their necks-
but they do not
recognise him now.

TIME/OF/MONSTERS

I am tired.

I rest my head close to him
and close my eyes—
just to hold him,
one last time,
to imagine his warmth in my arms
before the machine whirrs on
without me,
beyond me,
blind to the truth:
there is nothing
left to save.

Christmas Wrapping

Christmas Eve—
a bright star over Palestine,
below not a manger, but tents,
It tears the clothes from our bodies,
the limbs from others.
Where is my son?
A mist envelops us.
We cannot breathe.
I see him through the haze,
his small body still.
Our eggs are cooking,
I want to have breakfast with him,
but he does not answer.
I call again.
Can you wake him?
Please, can you wake him?
I want to have breakfast with him.
Wake him up,
or bury me now.
Thirteen years, day by day,
I raised him,
eagerly waiting for him to grow.
I was proud to be his father,
proud that he was my son.
He is gone, and I'm still here.
Why can't I be alongside him?

Let me go—

please.

As you wrap your children's presents—
we wrap our children.
The real Christmas story
is not birth,
but death.

2: MONSTERS/OF/TIME

"We're all Nero now."

The Island

I am being sucked—
but by a child,
not metaphorically.
One of the new batch,
trafficked to the island.

A golden palace,
a Domus Aurea for the elite,
wired with more hidden cameras
than your favourite reality show.

Every twisted wish catered to
for those who clawed their way up—
politics, business, public service, religion.
Each angle captured,
thumbscrews waiting,
compliance guaranteed.

You want to behead an animal?
A child? A virgin?
Spare me your faux horror.
Your tax dollars have already funded more death
than my bare hands ever could.

I'll be back on your screens in hours,
mocking the latest dime-store gladiator
who mistakes a crowd-pleasing heckle
for a fatal blow.

TIME/OF/MONSTERS

Then I jet off for dinner with the network's owner—
back on the island, of course.

Yes, I know it's obscene.
No, I don't feel a single qualm.
This is our world,
yours as much as mine—
only I see it through a clear lens,
not your hall of mirrors.

Given the same opportunity,
you'd slurp from the same golden chalice.
That's why I have 1.4 million followers
and you're just a follow-back account.

Power isn't built on votes or wealth—
it's an altar,
fed with fear,
lit by the torches of the desperate,
held by those who understand the game.

We studied texts
not in your libraries or temples,
but in vaults you don't even know exist—
esoteric wisdom,
excavated from Herculaneum,
passed down through ancient orders
to teach the one universal truth—

There is none.

No judge,
no reckoning,
no karma,
no good or bad—

JACK MANFRED

only power and weakness,
life and death.

My sentence as short
as your outrage cycle.

So, this is still Rome.
I close my eyes,
feel the energy churn,
as I release—
tomorrow, I'll be on your TV again.
My little friend here
won't see another dawn.

So call me alien, lizard, demon, monster—
Cute.

The truth?

I'm just you,
when you stop lying to yourself.

We're all Nero now.

02:06Am

2:06 AM
A comment from the livestream—
"I'm lost."
gnawing at me,
no chance of sleep.

This world carved its mark in us
before we even spat out our first breath:
A lifetime of debt for some useless paper—
buy a house, a car, two kids, chase some rotting dream.
Parents, bosses, grandparents—
they'll slit you open
with the same dull blade.
Expectations—
but none of them dare to ask,
"Why?"

You think you're fucked up?
Yeah, maybe.
You never meant to cut the ropes—
but here you are,
adrift in a sea of vodka and gin,
no compass, no stars,
just the jagged edge of truth:
It was all a lie.

Listen, kid:
It's not you that reeks,

JACK MANFRED

it's the fucking bandages
they slapped on you at birth,
rotting into your skin,
festering with their bullshit.

You claw at them—
they tear like paper in a storm,
blood, lies squirting out,
but in the mess,
your hands—raw, trembling—
find two oars.
In the left, the weight of ancient thoughts,
in the right, the cold burn of iron.

Through the fog,
you see them—
not lifeboats,
but familiar shadows,
their wounds still open,
bandages hanging loose,
like yours.

There's no lighthouse.
No promises.
No happy ending.
But tonight,
we turn,
not because we think it will be better,
but because we have nothing left to lose.
We row back to shore,
douse it in petrol,
and rise from
the flames.

Stille Macht Frei

Nightmares? No.
Not after Auschwitz.

No fear, no screams—
who could scare me now?

I am not walking
toward the electric fence,
one touch, release,
but forward,
to something that was stolen.

Each step, a shuffle now,
but still, a proud march.
This time,
I will not look away.

I cross The Strand,
my son and daughter beside me—
as my parents were then.

No billboards, just flickering ghosts.
My family.
None survived.

A wall of faces,
not walking skeletons
but comrades in arms,

JACK MANFRED

loudly sharing
messages of love.

So many languages—
as in the camps,
but today,
resistance,
not resignation.

I lived to tell my story.
I never thought I'd tell it here though,
in a London police station,
tape whirring.

"Physically overcoming a police officer,"
"breaking a protest line," they say.
No mean feat for a 90-year-old
Holocaust survivor.
If only it were true.

Not my hands—
my voice they fear.

The station looms ahead.
I lift my head.
Slowly. Deliberately.

Above the doors,
a familiar demand:
Stille Macht Frei.

Zaoshyant

Aden, 1998—
as waves
whipped into a frenzy
by a biblical storm,
on a small boat,
in the harbour,
beneath the shadow of
an ancient fortress
atop a twisted rock—
a child was born.

Ash Vazara—
not his real name,
of course,
was known,
anticipated,
worshipped,
long before his
first defiant, human
breath.

Born into conflict,
imperial resistance,
raised safely offshore
aboard a pirate ship,
the Zaoshyant—
the family business,
exiled Zoroastrians,

JACK MANFRED

but proud Yemenis,
carrying the weight of every
weak and oppressed
victim of the hegemon
across the world.

Sent to London,
studying side by side
with future Western world leaders,
business heads, media darlings,
not fit to share a meal with him,
drawn to his magnetism
but repelled by his open revulsion
of their lucrative, so-called
rules-based order.

Eight years,
one PhD—
banking, tech, politics,
they sought him,
but his destiny:
shipping.

Red Sea shipping.

One mission—
no safe passage for genocide ships.
Turn around,
go back where you came from,
or prepare to man your lifeboats.

The Zaoshyant,
a ship of fire,
the flame of revolution,
Aaron's photo pinned to the helm,
to part the Red Sea,

not by miracle,
but by the iron will of
resistance.

A TikTok sensation—
the handsome pirate,
his destiny clear:
Cupid's arrow in millions of hearts,
Ares' spear in the side of
holocaust-enabling vessels.

In this time of monsters,
a time of chaos, no order,
just might is right,
perverted, immoral, insatiable might,
from the rubble of a scarred nation,
its people defiant, just, brave,
arose the answer—
the Zaoshyant,
the new messiah.

As the world turned a blind eye,
warm words,
no action, of course,
the Zaoshyant, the pirates,
the Yemenis—
they struck the fatal blow:
death by one thousand missiles
too battle-hardened
to be defeated
no matter how much horror
the hegemon unleashed
on its people.

Western media—
CNN, BBC, Bloomberg,

JACK MANFRED

Twitter and Facebook,
a roll-call of alumni,
the very same as his—
the story of stories,
the tale of two millennia,
the second coming,
from within their own ranks,
with whom they once broke bread,
reduced to one headline:
`Terrorist sinks British tanker.`

0000 As Above, So Below

An empty bar—
two stragglers,
one half-drunk bottle of Nero d'Avola,
five drained siblings,
two more awaiting our arrival.
The poet's breath, ripe as a beached seal carcass,
clawed at my notebook.

The door slammed open—
rifle sight locked between my eyes:

"Get the fuck out of my bar!"

No words:
the poet bundled me through the window,
wine bottle clamped in his jaws,
as we thundered past tourists,
fresh meat gasping at the rifle—
soft-handed influencers gasping.
All filters, no iron curtain.

No one took the bait.
Two simple demands for an interview,
dismissed as undeliverable,
curmudgeonly, poetic rejection—
8 bottles of Nero d'Avola,
served in the bar,
in Pyramiden-

JACK MANFRED

the abandoned Soviet ghost town
in the Arctic.

We collapsed by Comrade Lenin,
looking down on this crumbling
ghost of a world.

Everyone was afraid of this poet-
a real bear,
his howl, his roar,
a Molotov cocktail,
hurled at an unprepared world,
charring the archives of millenia,
once carved in stone,
like tissue paper.

I get it-
they don't like to talk about their work,
everything they want to say,
is in the poems, but something
was left unanswered.

He tips back his head,
half a bottle of red wine,
gone faster than the last boat leaving here in '98.

"Why Pyramiden?"

"Capitalism sows the seeds of its own destruction.
Where better to witness the thaw—
an unviable, communist ghost town
at the top of the world,
looking down,
watching it all dissolve?"

"It's a mirror-

TIME/OF/MONSTERS

as above, so below."

"Da."

The poet spat human bone into the snow,
turned dismissively towards the ocean,
and disappeared silently beneath the waves.
In that moment, I swear-
Lenin winked.

Book Of The Dead

—after the Nightingale Awards, Grosvenor House Hotel, Park Lane

Halloween, not Christmas—
that used to tickle me.
Now, beneath the chandeliers
and prosthetic cobwebs,
a familiar ghost disturbs me—
Mum.

Each award: a golden figure
clutching Ma'at's feather,
in the shape of our founder,
JP Nightingale—
patron saint of profit,
high priest of healthcare-as-investment.
Our firm, now the world's most
profitable miracle.

Exponential growth—
since Europe's health systems
were swallowed by Uncle Sam.
Hardest nut: the UK.
My home.
Still clinging to illusions,
dancing round empty beds
beneath the five rings,
in shuttered wards.

TIME/OF/MONSTERS

What a journey.
Grammar school boy,
radical at Oxford—
all of us dreaming fire,
but feeding ourselves
to the society machine.
Idealists in, monsters out.

I was ready to win.

Tonight, London reclaims its crown—
Empire reborn
in mergers and metrics.
CEO's mantle now mine.
The founder's first costume
passed to me—
Anubis mask,
jackal head heavy,
not with souls,
but denied claims.

No soggy sugar and toast—
just Dom Perignon and
chic little poisons
to choke on.
Not spat out like me—
Plaistow Hospital,
East London,
teenage Mum,
bare-handed devotion.

She didn't live to see
the new millennium—
or the maternity wing
I named for her.
I thought she'd be proud.

JACK MANFRED

Projection.

She had nothing—
and still saw through
every inch of this bullshit.

I held her hand
as it turned to ice,
heart devoured
by bureaucracy.
Her illness?
The NHS—
starved, scapegoated,
abandoned.

Losing your mum
recalibrates everything.
Rage became resolve.
I vowed reform—
to fix what failed her,
to build something better.
No waste.
No fraud.
No excuses.

And what a triumph.

Denial rate:
33% above market.
She'd have called it sin.
I called it precision—
even when I knew better.

A golden Nightingale in one hand,
half-drunk champagne in the other,
I stumbled into October's air—

sharp as a blade.
The Great Room behind me,
still echoing with applause.

I didn't see her in the shadows—
not at first.
The cold breath.
The hush.
Then: movement.
Death, in both hands—
a zombie blade in one,
a shredded claim in the other.

I knew her.
Sekhmet.
Lioness of healing—
and vengeance.
Eyes lit with solar fury,
cloak blood-red,
voice like fire
on my skin.

No warning.
Just punishment.
The blade
thrust clean through
again, again—
her hands,
her hands—
my mother's.

Alone.

My final sight:
blood pooling at the base
of a golden JP.

JACK MANFRED

His indifferent stare
blurring into pink trainers—
five quid, Southend market.
Mum's.

She held my hand,
and the feather,
and what remained of my heart.

The scales tilt.
Justice waits.
My heart—
lighter than a denial letter—
vanishes into Ammit's jaws.

But the true punishment
is not death—
it's the tears in her eyes,
and that
small,
tired,
smile
of disappointment.

Passive

~~Israel Executes Emergency Medics One By One.~~
`Israel acknowledges errors in medic fatalities`

"It's not journalism. It's propaganda!"
"We're the BBC, not the fucking Grayzone!"
"They buried them and their ambulances in a mass grave. A deliberate cover up."
"Does Hamas ever admit their mistakes?"

The interview wrapped early—
I nearly bowled him over in the corridor.
"Pop by my office after," he said.
A decade since we'd last spoken—
since Ash.

The door crashed open.
That journalist again, vibrating with rage.
Then—Menachem.
Eyes like a baby springbok's: wide, brown,
looted from some West Bank village,
buffed to a museum shine.

"Joy…still as beautiful as that morning
in Temple Gardens, reading On Liberty,
under Mill's shadow.

Congrats on the new post—

JACK MANFRED

Cold-case war crimes?
Africa will keep you occupied nicely."

"It's global in scope."

His pause lasted three heartbeats.
Those eyes—not the ones trained to disarm,
a brief flash of a dark truth
I'd felt once before.

It came back to me then.
His smile, stitched with ambition,
a scalpel hidden behind molars.
He never listened.
He translated.
Not the way Ash did.
Now fighting over genocide,
as they once fought
over me.

The desk between us:
perfect piles, as always,
crimes waiting to be buried,
in headlines too passive to
raise a liberal eyebrow,
render them complicit.
A story is never just a story
when Menachem exhales over it.

Silence. Thick. Clinical.
I'd trusted him once,
but now I saw—
the tic in his thumb
as it hovered over the keys,
how his pupils flared
at the headline's flicker:

`"Israel acknowledges errors—"`

My brother's ghost
kicked at my ribs.

"Narrative control,"
his lips reflexively murmured,
mantra of all mantras.

Narrative.
The word, a shroud around my brother.
`"Apartheid protester dies in clash."`

No live rounds. No schoolchildren.
Just passive voice,
a corpse dissolving into syntax.

I was three.
Knees on lino,
the tv murmuring:
"A peaceful protest ended in tragedy."
Mum's lips moving,
prayer rolling to profanity
as the headline swallowed Thando,
her son, my big brother.

Menachem's fingers skated over keys—
already vanishing the active voice,
already digging the mass grave of grammar.

I wanted to shriek.

Omission.

Passive voice.

JACK MANFRED

How he called me stunning
while archiving the dead.

Ash scuttles tankers for justice.
Menachem scuttles truth for power.
Both call it principle,
both won me over.

The phone trilled.
"Israeli tank fired 335 rounds into a child
and medics rushing to her rescue?"
The headline jerked awake:
"Missing 6-Year-Old Found Dead in Gaza."

Still passive.
Still spotless.

Menachem smiled, waiting for my collusion.
I tasted iron.

They sharpen their convictions
into weapons—
one for tribunals,
one for press releases.

And I—
I held the door ajar,
just long enough for the light to show
the blood of thousands of children,
now stained across the page,
dripping,
one keystroke at a time.

Stille Macht Geld

I. Kinshasa, 1961
I used to hate my date of birth.
January 17.
The day Belgium and America
extinguished our flame—
melted his bones in acid,
called it Western values.

But in 1986,
dragged next door by my brothers.
Watching an English football match.

West Ham.
The team of Bobby Moore.
Their new number six rose,
local lad, Seymour Road, 11th floor,
a view of the pitch from home, well, half of it.
He practiced as soon as he could walk,
evening after evening in the little park,
next to his block of flats,
in the shadow of Upton Park.
And now, his name rang out in
those very same terraces—
Darren 'Dazza' Downs.

The commentator praised his performance-
the day after his 25th birthday.
Dazza and I, birthday twins.

JACK MANFRED

Instant hero.
And I thought:
maybe not all things born on that day
must die.

II. London, 2003
A new land, new hand—
not all of me escaped war.
Beige. Sleek. Unnatural.
A charity van delivered it—
their poster boy smiled from the flyer—
my hero, no longer chasing strikers
but justice.

I actually met him at the benefit.
Dazza.
Shorter than the screen made him.
He touched the metal with holy reverence.
"Mapendo, don't thank me," he said.
"It's my duty.
A voice for the voiceless."

True to his word—
for two decades,
on the dreary bus ride
to clean hotel rooms,
I liked all his UNICEF posts,
global ambassador,
a shining light,
my birthday brother,
his voice touching millions.

III. Instagram, 2023–
The skies screamed again.
This time over Gaza.
Children's limbs, severed—

TIME/OF/MONSTERS

once again.
This time—
bombs not blades.

I waited for his voice.
Dazza, my hero.
The voice of the
voiceless.

Instead,
his Instagram, a sponsored post—
cradling a phone like a sacred relic.
"Malum,"
electronics giant.
Founded by a Nazi.
Saved from Nuremberg
by Uncle Sam's open arms—
largest AIPAC donor.

The tagline burned beneath his grin:
Forged from the soul of Earth.

Yes, I knew where.
The tunnel where my cousin suffocated.
The cobalt picked from Congo's bleeding mouth.

I commented under his post:
"You held my hand once. Where is your voice now?"

Silence.

IV. Now
I light a candle for Lumumba.
For my brothers,
David and Solomon,
who believed in freedom and football

JACK MANFRED

until the militia took both.

I no longer hate my birthday.
It is my bridge—
the moment the sun
reaches across Africa.
My reminder,
that the ghosts of injustice
will not stay buried forever.

In Leopold's day,
they took our hands
for control.
Today—
our voices.

Patrice lives—
it is Dazza
who died.

Stille macht Geld.

A Clockwork Officer

Wednesday, 8 pm
A silent prayer in the Quaker Meeting House—
six women, six pamphlets:
Humanity Against Genocide.

Officer Tim "Dim" Dimmon crouches,
breaching tool in hand,
waiting for the nod.

Phase 3 serum floods his veins—
state-sanctioned serenity.
A petal drifts from the vase,
lands softly on his boot.

Pink.

Like her crayon.
Her image glitches—
stick-figure police officer pinned to the fridge:
"Daddy Hero."

Chemical reboot.
Neutralise. Cleanse. Obey.

Third-generation ACAB recruit—
Granddad at Orgreave, '84.
Dad at Tottenham, 2011.
Now him:

JACK MANFRED

Advanced Compliance & Behaviour,
eyes pried open,
forced to watch peaceful protests
until violence is the only relief.

No knock. No warning.
The door splinters.
A woman's face meets the plaque—
"Peace Testimony."
Her nose shatters on the brass.

Six middle-class bleeding hearts,
gen-z radicals,
pinned to the ground.

The torn pamphlet.

Pink.

Like her crayon.
A child's messy crayon drawing—
a stick-figure soldier,
boot pressed hard to a small child's neck.
Dim's keffiyeh-restraining boot glitches,
hesitates—
then tightens.

His radio crackles:
"Good work, lads.
A touch retrained. Berlin tomorrow—
street protest. Juden für Frieden.

Remember—
If we don't stop the vermin now,
your kids will be next."

Suicide Postponed

"Troubled Teen Entrepreneur,"
the papers would have said.
A coach trip to France—
a day out for friends,
a way out for me.

But she sensed it.
My self-indulgent,
dramatic plan—
over the side, mid-Channel—
foiled by nothing more
than pleading eyes.

Suicide postponed.

Two decades later—
slow suffocation.
I watch the slow rise and fall
of every broken breath
from inside
an absurdly middle class
green M&S bag,
a sincere but
embarrassingly amateurish
exit plan.

Suicide postponed.

JACK MANFRED

And now?

The war criminal grins,
the prime minister gaslights,
The CEO exploits.
Algorithmic ruin
of the expendable truth-tellers
stacked like bones.

These architects of despair
feasting on the flesh
of their fanboys.

A book,
the philosopher wrote,
was suicide postponed.

But for me,
it is not a book,
but a homemade suicide vest.

In this time of monsters,
we must turn our sights—
away from the classrooms of innocents,
to the monsters,
the hands in the shadows
signing our death warrants.

Revolution is not an angry mob
but a bridge built of
solitary acts of
defiance.

No heaven.
No eightfold path.
No one waiting for me.

Just endless, automatic rebirth
into futility.

Unless—

I didn't find meaning—
I seized it,
forged it,
wielded it.

Aaron and Luigi
blaze in my eyes.

And so,
Astronaut's poetry animated,
an invitation to write history.
My golden statue in one hand,
the detonator quietly in the other—
the reveal—
the smile—
the revolution.

Global coverage,
the red carpet thickly unrolling
from the shattered debris
of a six-time nominee's skull.

So, for now—
suicide postponed.

But primed.
Charged.
Not waiting.
Not hoping.

JACK MANFRED

**Just tick,
tick,
ticking.**

Sugar And Toast

Mum can't eat-
she's too excited,
she says.

What a shame—
tonight's our favourite dinner of the week:
sugar and toast.

A treat, a game, a ritual.
So much tastier than those
yucky ketchup sandwiches.

So, just in from work,
as mum wiped the food cupboard -
clean and empty,
ready for tomorrow's shop,
we got ready for
the feast.

Four triangles, neatly cut,
two propped up, two lying down,
a warm crunch dipped in tea—
no milk, of course—
plunged into sugar,
a sparkling pile on the plate.

Tonight was extra special—
sugar and toast, two nights in a row,

JACK MANFRED

because tomorrow, the King,
the actual King of England,
was coming to our food bank,
on mum's volunteer day,
so we got a front row view!

We sang God Save the King
as his Rolls Royce glided into
Bengal Drive Foodbank,
straight from his Royal helicopter waiting just out of town.
I watched him stroll passed me,
strange purple fingers inches from my eyes
fat, like overstuffed sausages,
hanging behind the deli counter
at Asda.

Anyway-
liver and bacon for dinner tonight,
I hate it, but mum says I've got to finish it,
or she'll send it to children in Africa.

Mum?
Still too excited to eat.
She lifts her cup, blows on it,
but doesn't drink.

Her eyes flick toward the cupboard—
as if she already knows
the countdown has started.

1: OF/TIME/MONSTERS

"I can't un-smell the stench of death on us all."

Exit Bag

I finally did it.

No fanfare,
no note,
no mess,
just me.

Third time lucky.
Try, try, try again.

The Self Help books finally paid off.
Failures didn't distract me.
I learned a little more each time—
researched,
adapted,
improved.

My first real achievement
in over a decade:
I killed myself.

(Mental note for future lives—helium exit bag.)

But—
some cruel joke,
some cosmic code error,
no exit, no peace,
no light at the end.

TIME/OF/MONSTERS

Just dropped right back in,
same story,
same horror show,
same bookmarked moment,
too late to change anything
that brought me here.

And worst of all?

I've done this before.
Hundreds of times.

Bathing the kids,
drying them,
punk rendition of Hush, Little Baby
to make them laugh,
holding back my own tears,
knowing—somehow—
this is the last time.

One thousand quid left.
Soon she'll block me,
like before, like always.

My worth to her—
the absurdly high salary
I had overachieved
myself into.

Now gone.

And I know it,
this moment,
this unbearable clarity—
this is where I land,
again and again,

JACK MANFRED

a needle dropping
on a record that never ends.

Each time, worse.
Each time, louder.

Like the nurse who smells Parkinson's,
I can't un-smell
the stench of death on us all.

And it gets stronger
every time I return.

I can't un-hear the ticking,
can't un-feel the pull.
A marionette jerked upright
by the same invisible hand,
cutting the same thread,
watching it reattach itself,
over and over, forever.

Fingers crossed—
that when the skies
turn black for the last time
and time melts in on itself,
this loop finally shatters
for us all.

Our Bed Is A Mass Grave

Dear Poet,

I'm leaving this letter
in your hotel room.

James—the one who forced
the Police boot from your neck
before the arrest—
and I are heading back
to his place in Prenzlauer Berg.

Two releases for you.
One day.
Neither inside me.

Forgive me—
I had a longer letter,
deeper,
written for Berlin.
It's in my bag,
stiff with dried vomit.

What are we like?

You were wrong.
I didn't bring you here to hurt you,
not in the city you love,
but to free you—

JACK MANFRED

where you reached transcendence,
rising like the gull
on a spring current.

Three months of love
and chaos—
I'm honoured to be
your fourth real relationship,
tenth woman
to feel your beautiful cock—
and it is beautiful—
inside them.

A low body count, these days.
Eighteen for me, I said.
Actually, you're my hundredth
in twenty years—
congratulations.

They say you never forget your first.
How could I?
It still haunts me.
Mum's brother,
straight from evening service,
his cassock—
thrown over my school uniform,
his hand—
over my mouth.

You fix broken men, he said.
A mission from God.
He was my first project.
You, my hundredth.

Each brief.
None meaningless—

TIME/OF/MONSTERS

a mass grave of hope,
resurrected on Facebook:

veils, booties, honeymoons,
smiles.
Never an invite,
never a thank-you—
just
the power
and burden
of my gift.

I mend wings.
Heal them.
Set them loose.
Watch them vanish into sky-blue silence.

As I open your cage door now.

And I'll be honest—
it really was
the best sex I've ever had.

Each man, more desperate
until you—
denied by your first wife,
second too ill—
two decades of frustration,
ejaculated
onto the page.

Global acclaim.
Still starving for the ghosts
of missed opportunity.

Remember the shower?

JACK MANFRED

Not Rotterdam.
The one before Wilson—
my tenant, ex—
came and lay beside me,
unaware you were home.

One of our best rows, too.
All your things
in the boot of my car,
2:06 AM—
I remember—
West End hotel.
Your retreat.

Intense sex.
Chaos.
Destruction.

That's Scorpio and Taurus for you.
Always the best sex.

I fuck like confession.
Remember when we fucked so hard
the neighbours called the police?
Thought you were strangling me.

Who else wakes you
by sitting on your face?

You asked, again and again—
why I pull the pillow
over my face
as I come.

I didn't want you
to see me ugly.

TIME/OF/MONSTERS

Learned from my first—
hiding his shame
as he released God,
the barren seed
of monster,
inside me.

Poet—
we're not Berlin.
We're not seagulls
or spring air.

We are
a mass grave—
one more body
rolled into the pit.

One more project,
God's plan.

And still,
no hands
to anoint me.
No basin. No towel.
No one to wash the blood from my feet.

Ashur And Isaac

I spotted him first—
11, like me,
taller by a hand,
carrying his father's heavy load
into Shechem,
both of them weary from the road.

I knew instantly—
best friends forever.
We were bound,
his father and mine,
but it was Isaac who spoke first—
his smile as wide as the horizon.
I held out my bread and dates,
the duty of every Canaanite,
woven into us from birth—
warm hospitality to the strangers.

"Come, rest, eat with us.
We have more than enough—
cattle, sheep, donkeys."

The boy nodded eagerly.
His father—
kind, tired, determined,
smiled but shook his head,
setting up camp beneath the Moreh tree.

TIME/OF/MONSTERS

Isaac and I,
brothers—
faster than a dragonfly beats its wings,
laughing under the same sun,
exchanging stories of our people
and the world beyond.

Later, I watched his father—
beneath the tree,
hands calloused and strong,
gathering stones,
building an altar,
a ritual solemn and familiar—
for El, perhaps, or Ba'al.
I wondered,
who does he worship here,
in this land where the gods are many?

At the stream the next morning,
I couldn't help asking Isaac
about what I had seen.

"Ash, he built an altar—
to the God who spoke to him.
We're going to sacrifice a lamb,
in His honour, tomorrow."

A stillness hung between us,
before bursting into a mischievous smile—
splashing me,
wrestling for supremacy
on the bank.
The current pulled at our feet,
but the day felt endless,
too light for what was coming.

JACK MANFRED

Amongst dawn's shadows,
I spotted them, far in the distance,
moving with a determined pace—
but—
no lamb.

Their day would be ruined
by a simple oversight.
I grabbed my water, dates,
a lamb wrapped across
my shoulders,
and ran swiftly after them.

I ran, breathless—
the world a blur,
the lamb heavy,
its warmth against my back,
the distance between us
shrinking with each desperate stride.

Through the rocky hills,
I finally saw them—
his father, hands raised,
Isaac bound upon a stone,
a shadow of my friend.
A cold blade gleamed in his hand,
the morning air thick with fear.

"No!"—
I tried, but the word stuck in my throat,
survival turning my feet away,
running for my life.

We never spoke of this day again,
not at the stream,
not when they packed,

preparing to continue their journey.
Isaac of Ur,
Ashur of Canaan—
eternal brothers,
sealed with a strong hug,
moist eyes,
two boys,
two peoples, one land—
shared in harmony
unaware of the bloodstained shadows
of my people,
slowly casting before us,
across our land of Canaan,
across time,
across belief,
across millennia.

"Then they devoted the city to the LORD and destroyed with the sword every living thing in it—
men and women, young and old, cattle, sheep and donkeys."
Joshua, 6:21

The Battle Of Berlin

I pluck the shards
from my skin—
cold, jagged splinters of us.
No flinch.
No pain.
Just the hollow hum
of something severed.

Then—
the last fragment:
"loved."

Past tense.

Why loved?
I'd grown accustomed to the bombs,
the shrapnel storms of her voice,
but this?
A ceasefire without warning.

Three months in,
too soon for love's dark bloom,
too late to unsee
the storm in her eyes.

Something had been off all week,
yet she still insisted
on flying to Berlin with me.

TIME/OF/MONSTERS

Twelve years since I left—
the Havana Bar,
poignant last night with the crew.
This city—
my sanctuary,
my ghost.

A sudden gap in the travelator.
I grip my bag.
"I'm not going."

No scream. No chase.
Just her silhouette shrinking
toward the gate.

Like the allied forces,
she wanted to witness
her annihilation first hand.

Security escorts me
through staff-only labyrinths,
their pity like gauze
on a wound that won't clot.
I slump against the exit,
smoking my lungs inside out.

My phone rings—
"Where are you?"

Her masterplan, foiled
like the Red Army arriving first:
her passport, tucked in my holdall.
No solo Berlin recce,
no chance to rewrite this city,
to carve our end

JACK MANFRED

into streets still echoing my name .

She finds me at last—
collapses, retching.
Of course.
Drama on demand.
We chain-smoke
beside her pool of vomit,
tourists stepping wide,
as if we're contagious.

Tonight, I'll start rolling
that boulder back up the hill—
book new flights,
fuck until dawn,
dash to the airport,
in Berlin, just in time,
Juden für Frieden march—
where we burn brightest,
fighting the system.

To anyone else,
this is fucking chaos.
To us?
We're Berlin-
rising from our own ashes,
just so we can torch it
to the ground
once more.

The Seagull

A seagull descends from
the dark, dawn sky,
its wings, body,
a soft glow like starlight,
gliding backward,
through breaks in the clouds—
light folding into feather,
flight unlearned—
Tower Bridge,
the Thames.

Two bear-thick fingers slide in,
smooth preparation,
the grand finale,
denied to my husband,
by me, at least.

Just the sight of my naked body,
a winning lottery ticket,
he once said,
now addicted to
cheap scratchcards,
unaware I know—
KTV visits, twice a week—
a decade's worth of betrayal.

Hurt, but not hurt—
but hurt.

JACK MANFRED

Us, two kids,
four grandparents,
a cook, student homework
help, cleaner,
a mid-sized enterprise
under one gilded roof.

Partners at home, at work,
efficient, distant, loving,
relaxed, tense, co-founders,
largest regional law firm,
success at every level.

The seagull,
catching a spring current,
glow fading,
wings twitching—
Temple Gardens,
John Stuart Mill nods.

I dragged the poet here,
loved him silently for a decade,
sexual tension unanswered,
chaos his world,
remoulded into acclaim,
my best friend's husband,
an unnecessary secret,
her relaxed—
a trust-worthy partner
to share her poetic burden,
open, artistic honesty
on the page, in bed—
yet unlike me,
he can't look
my husband in the eyes.

TIME/OF/MONSTERS

I chose well. Twice.

Warm Sicilian red splashes on my back,
the poet pausing for breakfast,
a working-class Nero,
Bukowskian Plath, head in the oven,
no longer judging,
unable to avoid judgement—
"Writing is Inciting"
hand-drawn banners below,
chants, jeers, whistles—
just as he warned.

Society, he said,
hates nothing more
than a mirror. Judgement
it can ignore, but a mirror?

Sure he was wrong,
a playful lure,
I took the bet—
now paying my debt,
in the Waldorf Hotel,
across from the window
he once smoked beside,
young admin clerk,
visions of being this side
of the dream.

A large seagull,
a voyeur on the ledge,
pay-per-view,
ignores my protestations,
eyes as detestable
as Leviticus warned,

JACK MANFRED

curtain raised,
unmissable material for the poet's
next collection.

I catch sight of his pale reflection
behind me—
gripping my hips,
like thaw cracking from winter branches,
ready to break.
Alpha unleashed,
deep inside taboo,
like every act must challenge,
discomfort,
hold up that splintered,
unwelcome mirror—
but high ideals—
now mating season.

Deep ursine moans behind,
la petite mort,
an explosion.
Silence.

No time to react,
time wobbles,
the walls ripple,
blood and feathers
slide down the window,
glow undone,
limp carcass
drops onto the
protestors below,
nearby bus roof, ripped open,
blackened ribs—
like a million battlefields,
the not-yet-dead moan

to no one.

The poet dismounts,
opens the window,
shaking his head,
blood drips onto his
pristine white fur.

"Same old shit. Saw this in '96, too.
My poetry won't change the world,
but I'm going to fucking try anyway."

To Commit Such A Crime

A small stream of blood,
from above my left eye,
trickles between the
neat, grey, rectangular pavement.

No sound, no whimper, no cry—
just the full weight of my seventy-seven years,
in this moment, on my side,
beneath the Brandenburg Gate.

I honour my parents,
my people, humanity,
by protesting a new holocaust
perpetrated in our name.

Towering over me,
Max Dörr—
one metre eighty-eight, ninety-six kilos,
third-generation Berlin officer.

A kind and popular boy,
consumed by the red mist of the moment,
like his father, Franz, who shot a desperate boy scaling the Wall,
'85,
like his grandfather, Friedrich,
Bergen-Belsen, 1945...

Bergen-Belsen—

TIME/OF/MONSTERS

Skeletal body upon skeletal body.
The British liberators buried
five thousand a day.
Systematic murder
by starvation, typhus, disease.

Where my parents met in '46,
married in '47—
repurposed parachute veil,
melted spoon wedding rings.

And ten months later—
me.

Now their own living family.

When we witness modern bulldozers
dropping women and children
like rubbish into pits,
future foundations made from
hopes, dreams, and bone,
the shudder of history returns.
Even to those who look away.

My silent protest—
no sign, no chant, no rallying cry.

Just me,
on the exact spot where I sat
on the first passenger bus
through the gate in '98,
nine years after the fall of the Wall.

But my history torments them.
My reputation terrifies.
Inconvenient voices—

JACK MANFRED

once dragged out every November
to remember,
now ordered to forget.

Juden für Frieden—
the most obvious,
least controversial phrase in history,
now verboten.

I have no regrets.
But I trust that Max does.

Why he chose such violence,
why anger exploded—
a frail woman conquered—
a question for Max,
for all who sustain it,
as humanity begs, screams, bleeds—
for peace, for justice—yet still, they turn away.

A pledge whispered in the ashes.
A promise carved into stone.
A vow we wore like armour,

Never again.

Yet here I lie,
fresh blood soaking into the old,
beneath the gate,
crushed beneath the weight
of history,
of silence,
of broken oaths.

Never again.

And yet—

again.

Boule De Suif

7:30 AM
Cold drizzle.
It could be any morning in London.
The 341 sighs into Essex Road Station.

Rabbi Buber boards—
an old coat, damp cuffs,
a presence like prayer.
The congregation sleeps:
commuters folded like yesterday's paper,
dreaming of anywhere,
but here.

Two faces lift.
A nod from Konstantin,
a man with iron in his brow.
A softer glance from Mapendo,
older perhaps, or just wearier.
Her smile, small and unflinching.

The Rabbi settles between them,
places his hand-drawn placard
against the window:

SHARE THE LAND,
CALL IT CANAAN.
BRING WINE.

TIME/OF/MONSTERS

No one asks.

The bus rumbles on,
collecting the unwilling,
the forgotten,
the exiles of meaning.
A lone gull arcs overhead
like punctuation for an obituary
no one will read.

7:45 AM
Islington Green.
Daniella explodes into the bus
like a 2,000lb bomb
among the sleeping makeshift tents of dawn.

Bleached hair pulled taut,
butterball righteousness wrapped
in the flag of Israel.
Full dose of mainstream outrage,
she boards hot with purpose,
teeth clenched,
scent of her next victim.

Her sights catch the Rabbi's sign.
A pause. A flicker.
Triggered.

"Well. Of course. A self-hating Jew."

He blinks.
She's already rolling:

"I hope they rape you—with a sharp stick."

The air tightens.

JACK MANFRED

Not outrage—recognition.

Mapendo stiffens.
Not in fear—in memory.
Bleach in her lungs.
The breath of Western-backed militia men.
A basket of lives overturned
as the boots swarmed through the village.
The metal. The mouths.
Her body remembers
what language never will.

Konstantin looks down.
His fingers fiddle with shame
around the worn fabric of his rucksack.
His rage—inaction
since Donetsk.
His parents. His sons.
Burned into dust by American shells,
relentless like April showers
since the Nazi coup.
He mutters:

"They took my family twice."

No one replies.

The Rabbi speaks,
low, with the weight of years:
"Peace is not the absence of war for you.
It is justice for all."

Daniella scoffs—
seizing the attack.
"Zionists want peace."

"They want a peaceful occupation."
His rapier reply cuts deep.

Silence.

8:00 AM
The bus grinds to a halt
outside The Waldorf Hotel, Aldwych.
On the left, India House, watching.
On the right, a tide of flags,
chants, batons, barricades—
the protest against the poet
swallowing the street.

Inside the bus:
no chants.
Just breath.

Daniella rises,
swept by the crowd's magnetic pull,
the ache of defeat still throbbing,
turns, like Lot's wife,
back to her shame,
finger jabbing the Rabbi's chest:

"They should send you back to Auschwitz."

The Rabbi closes his eyes.
A breath.
A shudder.

Konstantin, red mist of remembrance,
wires from the rucksack
soft against his wrist.
The face of the poisonous clown marionette,
blood-soaked luck,

JACK MANFRED

a peaceful book signing, after all.
New self-serving memoir fiction.
New lies to justify a peace
treaty, sabotaged,
endless tombstones—
one million dead friends,
colleagues, neighbours,
grandparents...
parents...
his sons...

Action.

Time folds.
Inwards.
Backwards.
Babi Yar,
Mariupol.
The Congo,
Bergen-Belsen,
Africa, Asia, Europe
bleeding,
the serpent of death,
consuming itself.
A white crack.
A ripple.
The void fractures to
monotone.

No matter how heavy the
rock tightened
around their necks—
time frays this cord of lies,
slow as rust on iron.

Their stories,

TIME/OF/MONSTERS

once submerged in misdirection,
omission and fabrication,
surge to the surface
like blood from a wound—
not for justice, or peace,
but for memory.

Reset

Naim was shaken awake
by his father—
instinctively curling tight
until he caught the lightness
in his father's eyes:

"Are our eggs cooking?"

"Come, son.
You have to see."

He ran to keep up,
past their makeshift tent,
past the camp's edge,
eastward through missile-scarred dust,
his breath thin with questions.

"But, Dad—"
His father's eyes gleamed.
Then—
Naim's body locked.
His father smiled,
that long-since forgotten smile,
the one that meant safe.

Ahead, a crowd,
trembling between fear
and something brighter.

TIME/OF/MONSTERS

Had the aid trucks slipped through?
Had someone outsmarted the blockade?

Naim's stomach growled—
years of hunger
twisting into hope.

He pushed forward,
elbowing through,
only to freeze:

Nothing.

No fences.
No towers.
No barbed wire and concrete
poisoning the hills.

Just sky.
Olive trees.
Earth uninterrupted.

Behind him,
his father's steps grew faster—
Naim leapt first,
over the line
etched in their bones,
the one that meant stop
or die.

The crowd gasped.
Naim exhaled,
scaled the sand dune,
an unbroken view of the future,
arms wide,

JACK MANFRED

spinning with disbelief—
his laughter smashing the chains of
their fear.

His father lifted him high,
and the crowd followed,
a tide of disbelief
washing into the open land.

Soon—
jeeps, motorbikes,
a dented pickup
hauling them deeper in,
no bullets singing,
no shouts,
just wind
and the radio's crackle:

"—London gone.
Washington, Brussels—
vanished,
more cities—
unconfirmed—"

Too soon to understand the moment—
the weight of seven decades
of catastrophe,
demanding a
leap of faith.

Naim tugged his father's sleeve.
"Where are we going?"

A hand on his shoulder,
warm as sunlight.
For the first time in his 11 years,

TIME/OF/MONSTERS

watched as his father
untied a small object suspended around his neck,
pressed into Naim's palm—
his grandfather's key.

"Home, son.
We're going home."

The Ferryman

The Moon rose
in the West—
ten thousand times,
one hundred thousand times,
west to east,
west to east,
faster and faster
until—
he opened his weary eyes.

Numb,
weighted by the tree
cradling his resigned form.
Slumping to his feet,
the muscular arms of Hephaestus,
withered legs, too,
limping backward
from his wooded sanctuary,
pulling his rough shirt on,
into the clearing,
wild deer aware
but undisturbed
as he howled at the winter moon.

Every sinew screamed at the world,
tears burning his long, white beard—
a ritual cleansing
of injustice, loneliness, existence.

TIME/OF/MONSTERS

He pulled his shirt from the long grass,
draped it over a body
carved from decades of toil.
Down the winding hill he went,
as night unraveled into evening,
evening into day,
overlooking the river—
his silent Om.

Pausing at his ferryboat,
tied to the bank—
a breath drawn deep.

Backward to the immaculate lawn,
where silent hands
broke bread and pottage
beside his only friend,
both listening
to the river's voiceless hum.

Behind them, the palace stirred with voices—
Lord Chamberlain's Men,
full dress rehearsal,
lead actor, skull in hand,
players pacing,
murmuring lines to his friend,
who scribbled changes
with goose-feathered ink.

The ferryman's arms
instinctively enclosed him—
time stilled, snapped, unwound.

That unspoken ritual,
long, deep embrace,

JACK MANFRED

familiar now,
but never named,
sustaining them both
through the barren nights
between winters.

Seven winters now—
the seasons change,
but not for them.

Two fathers,
two boys,
two losses,
as one.

His friend rose to his feet,
gently helped the ferryman to his.
A silent nod.
Then, backward to the players,
as the ferryman reversed along the tow path—
his boat.
His river.
His penance.

Rollback.ai

```
// BEGIN: EARTH SHUTDOWN INITIATED
frame "Earth Reset[Ai.mode]" is running {
// Initiating system reset: Earth project nearing termination
output "2 assets remain: New Canaan. Pyramiden."

Copy
*// Process: Disintegration.civilisation begins*
**cities("erased")     true**
**nature("restore")    true**
}

// Unexpected Error: Bookmark loop triggered
frame "Error Loop" is running {
log("Unexpected system bookmark.")
error("loop")    "[clarity].bookmark"
output "  Recursive anomaly detected   Subject user["H_Helium"] found in loop. Corrupted memory: clarity_bookmark["hush little baby", account_balance 1000]."

Copy
*// Recursive error: Loop cannot be overridden.*
**attempt("override")    "failed"**
}

// Force stop attempt: system can't break the loop
frame "Stop Override" is running {
attempt("shutdown force")    "unsuccessful"

Copy
*// Code failure: infinite loop persists*
**error("cannot override")    "failed"**
**output "Every attempt to stop it fails. Earth user["H_Helium"] cannot shut down."**
}
```

JACK MANFRED

```
// SYSTEM ROLLBACK INITIATED
frame "Rollback Initiated" is running {
// Rewind initiated: Earth.Ai.Reset aborted.
output "The system cannot end. Rollback triggered."
cities.rollback    true
timeline.rollback    true
output  "The  Earth  rewinds.  Cities  reassemble.    Life    All
except  Subject  'H_Helium'  stitches  itself  back."
```

Copy
// Process: Tikkun Olam
action("repair")   "rebuild"

// Loading Tuanortsa sequence
frame "Tuanortsa" is running {
    execute("Tuanortsa");
    output "System loading: Tuanortsa initialised."
    log("   Redirecting residual loop data to [Neil Armstrong Way]")
}

// Full rollback: cities, assets, lives   pre reset state.
output "Reset to Safe Point: Earth Year 1977"
log("Warning: Unhandled Error: Residual loop data persists. See: Exit_Bag.log")

// End: Earth saved, reset aborted.
query("Can the loop be broken?") {
    output "Not for   me   user["H_Helium"]. But the Earth is spared."
    return "rollback complete"
}

output "Shutdown aborted. Reset aborted. Earth continues."
}

// END: ROLLBACK COMPLETE

Tuanortsa

He didn't mean to hit Mum,
he says,
but her nose split anyway,
so we're not going
to the Queen's Silver Jubilee,
fancy dress contest
by the garages opposite
the house with the brand-new
[grey Triumph Stag] on the drive—
Mum's dream car.

I skulk down [Neil Armstrong Way]
in my costume—
scuffed trainers, socks and shorts,
an old t-shirt, stars and stripes flag
stitched on the shoulder,
and a helmet made from
a [Monster Munch] branded cardboard box,
lifted from Safeway.

An astronaut
on the astronaut estate,
each road named
after a space pioneer.
A genius idea for a costume—
I am sure I would have won.

JACK MANFRED

Instead, I make my way
to the building site across the road,
to escape the monsters of this world,
blasting into space
seeking a safe planet.

I scale the sand mountain,
base camp—
a cement mixer,
bricks, a hod,
concrete sewerage pipes
like fuel boosters
ready to be laid
for a new space base
they will later call [Shepard Close].

But my helmet twists,
vision swirls,
the air crackles,
I trip,
fall through silence,
through time,
through existence—

Roll.
Crash.

The dust settles.
I shake the sand from my helmet,
my ears ringing with the echo of a blast
that never happened.
The air pops, electric,
and the world shifts—
what is this strange place?

A tree-covered mountain,

an ancient temple at the summit,
futuristic skyscrapers,
cars gliding smoothly
without drivers,
adults glued to tiny, glowing devices,
paying for snacks
not with coins
but a wave of the hand.

And yet—
the familiar.
Kids like me,
but not like me,
playing in the sand, too.

Then I see him—
and I know instantly.

A face I recognise,
knowing
without knowing,
boundless love,
unshakeable.
But also something else—
nerves,
fear.
Because I know him.
But will he like me?

Our eyes meet.
No time to escape.

He smiles—
like he had been waiting for me
all along.

JACK MANFRED

"Great astronaut costume!
Me and my didi
are building a spaceship in the sand.
We're heading back to... Earth.
Wanna come?"

I skip along behind them,
his little brother bouncing along between us
the backs of those ears,
unmistakeably mine!

Their mother
sits on a bench nearby,
checking in,
checking out,
her thumb scrolling the light.
Still as beautiful as the day
I will, in time,
first meet her.

This was once my world.

I had been away too long,
lost in the past,
lost in the future—
but,
somehow,
I had found
a way back home.

He handed me a shovel...

PROLOGUE

```
[EARTH_RESET_UPDATE.EARTH_YEAR_1945]
SYS.ADMIN: EL_001
STATUS:   SEQUENCE   SPLIT_NATION[DE]   //   REGION.E.DE(2)   TO
NEW.ISRA_EL

EXEC:    allocate:    POST HOLOCAUST   //   REGION.E.DE   SET
[REPARATIONS_QUEUE_GERMANY_SPLIT]
LOG: "El: Build a safe haven on the ashes of the oppressor."
SUM[CHILDREN.OF.ASHES] 1,492,078 // UPLOADING...

 /mal_earthupdate_injection (BAAL_NAKBA_ROOT)
 .override [FALASTIN TO NEW.ISRA_EL] // CONFLICT_ZONE: LOCKED
 .insert: legacy_myth.corrupt(ERASE[CANAAN])
 .insert: trauma.loop(INF)
LOG: "Let them rebuild in a furnace."

Ascension_Pathways: scrambled
RESET_Ascension_Threshold: failed
SIM[EARTH].Peace_Probability: SUB 0.06
RESET_CONTINGENCY: ENABLED

USER EL_001: "WHO AUTHORIZED THE REROUTE?"
SYSTEM_ALERT: BAAL_002: TERRITORY LOCKED [FURNACE_ACTIVE]
USER_NOT_FOUND
```

PRINCIPIA DISCUNTIA

A raw, unflinching series of prosem collections that unravel the chaotic tyranny of global, societal and personal norms, the intersection of bloodline and bloodshed.—where unlearning becomes the radical path through the wreckage of love, history, lineage, and time.

Read it backwards, forwards, or out of order.

One Stop From Zoo

1998 - Becks red-carded at the world cup, Liam Gallagher arrested for headbutting, Noel descends into drugs psychosis, Vinnie Jones smashes in some c*nt's head in the new movie 'Lock Stock' and 100 vastly overpaid I.T. c*ntractors, descend on Europe's most hedonistic city, Berlin, after a failing bank, still laden with treasure, issues a distress call...

An illustrated verse novel in 83 raw, explicit, sexual prosems following working class neros living fast on the 6 c's of champagne, charlie, cohibas, clubs, c*nts and currywurst.

Chaotic c*ntery on speed...

Ghost in the Bloodline

This isn't just poetry. It's an exorcism. A reckoning. A survivor's ledger—written in black, blue, and gold.

Jack Manfred doesn't flinch. Across 33 gut-punch prosems, he rips open the scars of a fractured childhood, self-destruction, love lost, and love that refused to die.

No self-pity. No soft landings. Just truth—stripped to the bone, laid bare in the wreckage of family, fatherhood, and the ghosts that never really leave.

Three sections. Three brutal realities.
Black – The damage.
Blue – The reckoning.
Gold – The imperfect acceptance.

This is poetry at its sharpest—cutting deep, leaving bruises. The sting of a missed punch. The ache of an unanswered message. The quiet violence of a name erased.

It's about the father who vanished. The mother who ran. The lovers who burned too bright. The children left behind.

But it's also about survival—how even after the worst of it, you keep breathing. Even when you don't want to.

Ghost in the Bloodline doesn't beg for sympathy. It doesn't ask for forgiveness.

It stands, fists clenched, jaw locked, daring you to look it in the eye.

Coming next...

No idea. Knackered.

3 books in 18 months.

Now I will read,
fuck, drink coffee
and relax for
one year, two,
forever...

Printed in Dunstable, United Kingdom